Eyes

Injury, Illness and Health

Carol Ballard

Heinemann
LIBRARY

www.heinemann.co.uk/library
Visit our website to find out more information about **Heinemann Library** books.

To order:
☎ Phone 44 (0) 1865 888066
📄 Send a fax to 44 (0) 1865 314091
💻 Visit the Heinemann Bookshop at www.heinemann.co.uk/library to browse our catalogue and order online.

First published in Great Britain by Heinemann Library, Halley Court, Jordan Hill, Oxford OX2 8EJ, part of Harcourt Education.

Heinemann is a registered trademark of Harcourt Education Ltd.

Editorial: Sarah Eason and Georga Godwin
Design: Jo Hinton-Malivoire and AMR
Illustrations: David Woodroffe
Picture Research: Rosie Garai and Debra Weatherly
Production: Viv Hichens

Originated by Blenheim Colour Ltd
Printed in Hong Kong, China
by Wing King Tong

ISBN 0 431 15701 4
07 06 05 04 03
10 9 8 7 6 5 4 3 2 1

British Library Cataloguing in Publication Data
Ballard, Carol
Eyes. – (Body Focus)
612.8'4
A full catalogue record for this book is available from the British Library.

Acknowledgements
The Publishers would like to thank the following for permission to reproduce photographs:
Actionplus pp. **10**, **37**; AKG London/Private Collection p. **41**; Bubbles/Moose Azim p. **6**; DK p. **11**; Getty Images pp. **7**, **9**, **27**, **40**; John Walmsley p. **29**; Popperfoto/Reuters p. **43**; SPL pp. **8**, **33**; SPL/Adam Hart-Davis pp. **25**, **34**; SPL/Argentum p. **39 (bottom)**; SPL/CC Studio p. **35**; SPL/Custom Medical Stock Photo p. **21**; SPL/Martin Dohrin p. **16 (bottom)**; SPL/Paul Parker p. **39 (top)**; SPL/Sue Ford p. **38**; The Wellcome Photo Library p. **42**; Trip/ A. Gasson p. **16 (top)**; Trip/A. Tjagny-Rjadno p. **14**; Trip/H. Rogers p. **19**.

The cover computer-enhanced image of the iris of an eye is produced courtesy of Science Photo Library/David Parker.

The Publishers would like to thank David Wright for his assistance with the preparation of this book.

Every effort has been made to contact copyright holders of any material reproduced in this book. Any omissions will be rectified in subsequent printings if notice is given to the Publishers.

CONTENTS

Words appearinng in the text in bold, **like this**, are explained in the glossary.

INTRODUCTION

Our eyes are the most important tools we have for collecting information about the world around us. Without our sense of sight, ordinary living becomes much more difficult.

We have two eyes, situated at the front of the face, protected by the bones of the skull. The bony hollow in which the eye sits is called the 'orbit', or 'socket'. Above, the hairy eyebrows help to prevent dust and dirt entering the eye. The rows of eyelashes also help to keep dust and dirt out of the eye, and the eyelids regularly sweep across the surface of the eye. Tears are produced, to keep the eyes moist and clean.

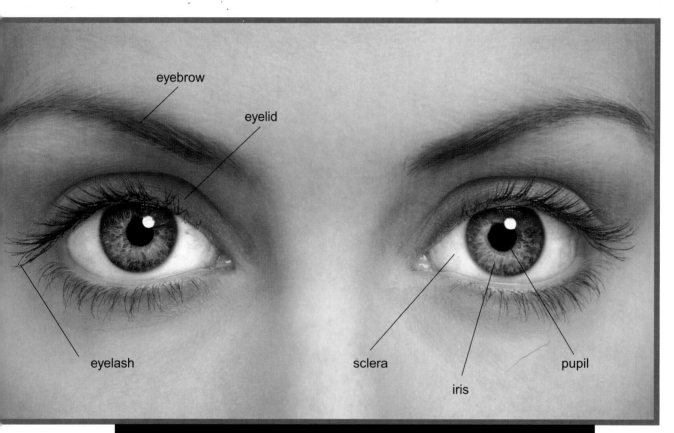

eyebrow

eyelid

eyelash

sclera

iris

pupil

Look at your eyes in a mirror. What can you see?

When you look at your eyes in a mirror, some features are very obvious. The white part of the eye is the **sclera**, and the coloured ring is the **iris**. Right at the centre is a black dot, the **pupil**. Although it may look solid, the pupil is actually a hole, and is covered by a transparent layer, the **cornea**. Light enters the eye through the pupil.

4

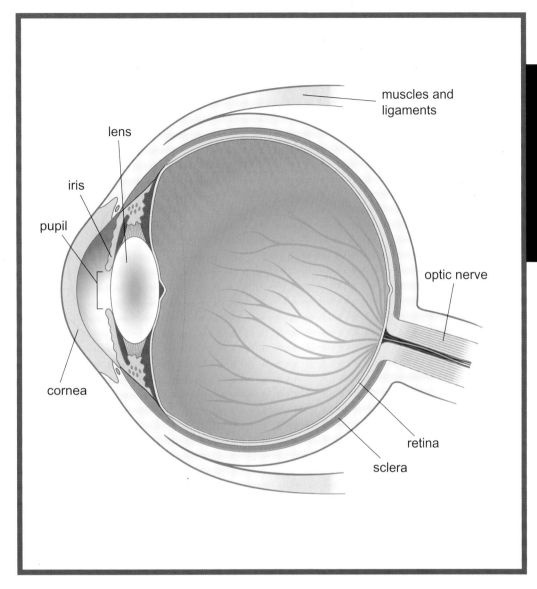

lens

iris

pupil

cornea

muscles and
ligaments

optic nerve

retina

sclera

This diagram shows the main structures inside an eye.

The eye is held in place by delicate muscles and **ligaments**. These allow us to move our eyes; the muscles of the two eyes usually work together, so that our eyes move together.

If you look inside an eye, you will find that there are two large spaces, called chambers. The one at the front of the eye is filled with a watery liquid, called the aqueous humour. Between the two chambers is a small disc of jelly, the **lens**. This bends the light as it enters the eye through the pupil. The larger chamber behind the lens is filled with a soft jelly, called the vitreous humour. The curved inner surface of the eyeball is lined with a light-sensitive layer, called the **retina**. The retina is linked to the **optic nerve**, which sends signals to the brain.

DEVELOPMENT OF SIGHT

When a baby is born, it is able to see, but its vision is not fully developed. Its sense of sight, its ability to focus and its ability to distinguish colours, shape and movements develop gradually during the first few months of its life.

At birth

The structures of the eye are fully formed at birth, but the pathways of nerves that carry signals from the eye to the brain are undeveloped. Light enters the eye and the baby will 'see', but it cannot make sense of what it sees.

Newborn babies can detect bright colours and big patterns. They can focus on things 20 to 30 centimetres from their eyes – roughly the distance between the baby's face and the mother's face when the baby is feeding. Within a week of birth, most babies can see their mother's facial expression.

First month

During the first few weeks of life, a baby is gradually able to distinguish between light and dark colours. It can distinguish between very different colours, such as yellow and blue, but cannot detect more subtle differences, such as different shades of green, or pale pink and pale blue.

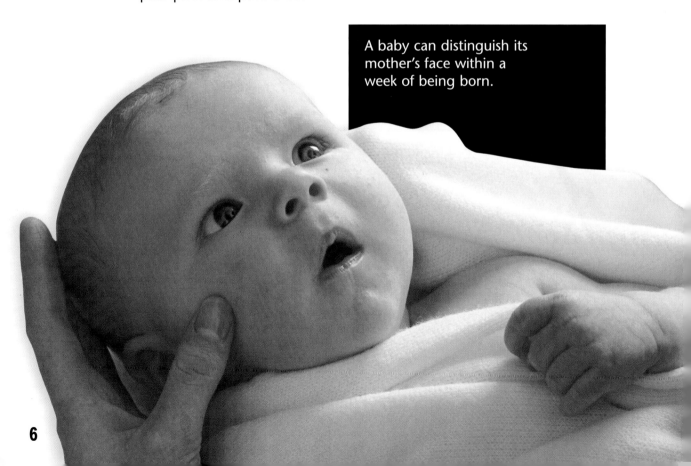

A baby can distinguish its mother's face within a week of being born.

Three months

By this time, most babies have learned to focus on things around them, and to follow something that is moving with both eyes. They blink if something is pushed towards their face. Their colour awareness has increased, and they are beginning to develop their hand/eye coordination – if they see something that attracts them, they are able to reach out and touch it.

By six months

Most babies are beginning to see as an adult does by the time that they are six months old. They can spot small objects, and can accurately track movements up and down, backwards and forwards and side to side. Their colour vision is fully developed, and they are getting better at judging distances. Although they can see things that are near to them more clearly than things in the distance, they are also able to locate and distinguish things at the far side of a room.

This one-year-old can follow objects moving away from him.

One year

In most children, the sense of sight is fully developed before they are one year old. They can focus near and far, judge distances, distinguish colours and track movements.

Eye problems

Within 22 days of conception, two shallow dips develop in the **embryo**. As the pregnancy progresses, the eyes will form at the site of these dips. The process of eye development is controlled by a series of **genes**. If any of these genes are abnormal, the eyes may not develop properly. Other problems may be caused by the mother being exposed to **viruses**. Some scientists think that chemicals, such as drugs and insecticides, environmental pollution and **radiation** may all be linked to babies born with deformed eyes, very small eyes or no eyes at all.

Eye checks

It is important to check that a baby's sight is developing properly – the sooner a problem is detected, the sooner it can be corrected. The first check is usually at birth, with a follow-up check at six months. The doctor needs to make sure that the two eyes are working together and that the baby is not near- or far-sighted. If necessary, spectacles may be prescribed, to help the baby to see and to ensure that both eyes work properly.

EYE CARE

Our eyes are very important to us and we should try to take great care of them. We can do this by wearing the correct eye protection, keeping our eyes clean, eating a healthy diet and visiting an **optician** regularly.

Protection

Eyes can be damaged in many ways. When we are doing any sport or activity that may lead to an eye injury, it is important to wear the correct protective equipment.

- Bright sunshine can damage the **retina** at the back of the eye. You should NEVER look directly at the Sun, and it is a good idea to wear sunglasses on bright, sunny days.
- Snow reflects a lot of light, and the glare can be as damaging to the eyes as bright sunlight. Too much exposure to glare from the snow can lead to 'snow-blindness'. Ski goggles should be regarded as an essential part of your ski equipment.
- Different sports present different hazards. Sportspeople, such as cricketers and ice hockey players, wear helmets with faceguards to protect their whole face, including their eyes, from a direct blow. If you normally wear glasses, and need them for sport, try to make sure that you have plastic lenses. Elastic straps can be attached to go round the back of your head to stop the glasses falling off as you move.
- Science laboratories and technology workshops can be dangerous places! Always wear the safety goggles provided to prevent splashes of liquid or solid particles getting into your eyes.
- Many jobs are best done wearing safety goggles or other eye protection. Welders wear full visors to protect their eyes from flying sparks, and many factory workers wear some form of eye protection to avoid eye injuries.

These children are wearing safety goggles to prevent splashes of acid and other dangerous chemicals getting into their eyes.

Clean eyes

Like any other part of your body, keeping your eyes clean reduces the likelihood of infection. Carefully wash away the 'sleep' that builds up around your eyes overnight and, if you wear eye make-up, always remove it daily. If you wear contact lenses, follow the instructions carefully, wearing them only for the prescribed time and using the correct washing solutions.

Food

The food that you eat affects your eyes. For healthy eyes, you need to eat a balanced diet. Make sure you include foods that are rich in vitamin A, such as carrots, eggs, fruit, leafy vegetables, liver and dairy products. These are important for eyes. The old wives' tale that 'carrots help you see in the dark' is true!

Computer monitors

Staring at a computer screen for long periods can make your eyes feel itchy and dry. Sometimes they may also feel hot and look red. This is usually because you don't blink often enough when using a computer. Try to take regular breaks, and give your eyes a rest every now and again by looking at something at the other side of the room for a few moments.

It is important to clean contact lenses very carefully, to avoid any dirt or micro-organisms getting onto your eyes.

Eye tests

It makes good sense to visit an optician for regular eye tests. Most of the time, you will probably be told that everything is fine – but if there is a problem, it is sensible to find out as early as possible.

If you already wear glasses or contact lenses, regular eye tests are even more important. Your eyes change with time, so your prescription may alter and need to be updated.

Bloodshot eyes

The clear layer of **membrane** that covers the white of the eye is usually colourless, and its tiny blood vessels are too fine to be seen. However, if the eye becomes infected or irritated, these tiny blood vessels may swell, and can be seen as the fine red threads of 'bloodshot eyes'. They usually return to normal slowly after the infection or irritation that caused them has gone.

Conjunctivitis

This is inflammation of the **conjunctiva**, the outer layer of the eye. It may be due to an infection or irritation, and can cause buildup of a sticky fluid, discomfort and watery eyes. Although conjunctivitis usually arises in one eye, it often spreads to the other eye, too. The treatment will depend on the cause of the inflammation.

Spots and floaters

It is quite common to see grey specks or threads that seem to be floating around in the eye. These are tiny pieces of debris that move slowly around in the jelly that fills the eye. These do not cause any harm although, in rare cases, they may indicate that the **retina** is damaged.

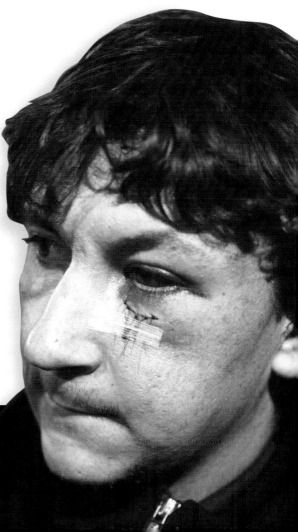

Scratched cornea

The surface of the **cornea** can be scratched by some accidental contact, such as a twig brushing against the face. The eye may feel sore and uncomfortable for a while, but this type of injury is rarely serious.

First aid for eyes

The main thing to remember about eye injuries is that you should let a doctor examine the injury as soon as possible. Stay calm and get expert advice!

This footballer has suffered a blow to the face, resulting in a black eye. The bruising will fade, but a visit to the doctor is necessary to ensure that there is no injury to the eye.

Black eye

This is not really an injury to the eye itself, but to the parts of the face around it. If there is a strong blow to the face close to the eye, blood and body fluid may collect in the area, causing bruising and swelling. Treatment as soon as possible with an ice pack can reduce the swelling, and the bruising usually fades in a few days. It is a good idea to let a doctor check the injury immediately to make sure there is no damage to the eye itself.

Grit in the eye

If you feel a speck of something in your eye, your immediate reaction is probably to rub it – DON'T! Try blinking a few times, but if the speck is still there, flush it out with lots of clean, lukewarm water. If this does not work, you should see a doctor for expert help.

Cut eye or eyelid

This is not something you should try to treat yourself – it will need immediate medical help. Do not put any pressure on the eye, and try to avoid rubbing it.

Flushing the eye with lots of lukewarm water will often help to remove any grit or other specks that may be irritating it.

Embedded object

If something has pierced the eyeball, DON'T try to remove it! Cover both eyes (to prevent the injured eye moving as the other eye moves) without putting any pressure on the injured eye. A small object would allow the eye to be covered with an eye patch or sterile dressing, but if the object is large, you may need to use something like a small cup. Get medical help as quickly as possible.

Chemical burns

First check the label of the chemical to make sure that it can be mixed with water without causing a harmful reaction. If it can, hold the eye wide open with your fingers and flood it immediately with clean, lukewarm water for at least fifteen minutes. Tell medical staff exactly what the chemical was, so that they can decide on the most effective treatment.

LOOKING AT EYES

We are all so used to seeing other people's eyes that you probably have not looked closely at your own for a while. Find a mirror and have a good, close look …

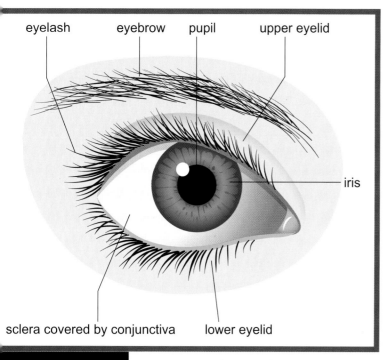

eyelash eyebrow pupil upper eyelid

iris

sclera covered by conjunctiva   lower eyelid

Can you identify all these parts of your own eyes?

Eyebrows

Eyebrows are thickened ridges of skin covered with short hairs. They jut out over the bone of the skull above the eye, protecting the eye from dust and debris. They stop sweat dripping down into the eye, and act like mini sun visors, helping to shade the eye just a little. They also act as shock absorbers, protecting the eye from blows to the head.

Eyelids

These are folds of skin that open at the front of the eyeball. They have four layers:

- an outer layer of skin, with hairs (eyelashes)
- a layer of muscle, which allows the eyelid to open and close
- a layer of fibres and oil glands
- a thin, transparent inner layer.

Eyelids protect the eye from dust and other foreign objects – as soon as something threatens the eye, a reflex reaction closes the eyelid. Eyelids also allow us to blink. As we blink, the eyelid spreads tears over the eyeball, keeping it moist.

Eye colour

Eye colour differs from person to person, and is determined by the amount of pigment (called **melanin**) present. Most dark-skinned people have a lot of melanin, so their eyes are dark. In pale-skinned people, eye colour can vary from very pale grey to blue, green and brown.

Iris colour is controlled by a single pair of **genes**. We get one gene from our mother and one gene from our father. The gene for brown eyes, **B**, is dominant and the gene for blue eyes, **b**, is recessive. This means that to have blue eyes you need two blue genes, **bb**. One brown gene and one blue gene, **Bb**, or two brown genes, **BB**, means you will have brown eyes.

Eyelashes

These are hairs that grow along the edges of the eyelids. Each eye usually has about 200 eyelashes. Each one lasts about 4 months before it falls out and is replaced with a new one.

Sclera and cornea

Together, the **sclera** and **cornea** make up the outer layer of the eyeball. The sclera makes up about five-sixths of the layer, and the cornea is about one-sixth. The sclera is a tough, fibrous **membrane**, and is the part we usually call the 'white of the eye'. It gives the eyeball its shape, and protects the structures inside the eye.
The cornea is transparent, and lies in front of the **iris** and **pupil**, making a slight bulge at the front of the eye. It has no blood vessels, and it bends the light a little as it enters the eye. The conjunctiva is joined continuously with the sclera.

Conjunctiva

This is a thin, transparent, **membrane** that forms the inner lining of the eyelids. It also covers the whole surface of the eyeball except the cornea. Because we need to move the eyeball, the conjunctiva is slack around the edges.

Iris and pupil

At the centre of the eye is a small black dot. This is actually a hole, called the pupil, through which light enters the eye.

Around the pupil is a coloured ring, the iris. This controls the size of the pupil, by opening and shutting.

These diagrams show the eye colours of children from different parents.

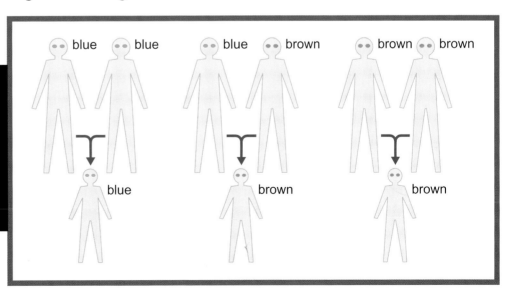

CORNEAL TRANSPLANT

The **cornea** is the transparent outer layer of the eye that covers the **iris** and **pupil**. If a person's cornea becomes damaged or diseased, they will not be able to see as well as they did previously. Corneal transplant now offers a way of restoring sight to people whose own corneas are damaged.

Corneal damage

Many things can lead to damage of the cornea, but some of the most common include:

- a serious infection by bacteria or **viruses**
- a chemical injury
- a cut or scratch of the corneal surface
- ageing.

Damage can affect the smooth surface of the cornea, its natural curve or its transparency. Any of these may lead to poor sight, and the need for a corneal transplant.

History

The first corneal transplant was carried out in 1906. Since then, advances in medicine have made it one of the most successful transplant operations. The cornea has no blood vessels, and therefore the white blood cells of the **immune system** cannot reach it and the body is very unlikely to reject the new tissue.

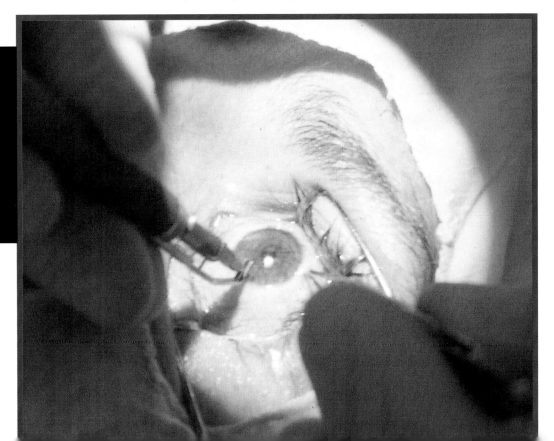

These doctors are carrying out eye surgery on a patient.

The operation

Although it has a very high success rate, the operation itself is very difficult. Surgeons work using a special operating microscope to magnify the eye 30 to 60 times.

The damaged cornea is cut with a circular blade with a hole in the centre – rather like punching out a circle of pastry with a pastry cutter. The damaged disc can then be lifted out.

The surgeon then cuts a disc from a healthy donated cornea, and places it carefully into the hole. This new disc of tissue is held in place by stitching it to the edges of the cornea.

The new cornea will allow the person to see clearly again within a couple of months of the operation, but the stitches need to remain in place for up to a year.

After the operation

Although the patient only needs to stay in hospital for a short while, they must take great care. Special drops need to be put into the eye to help it to heal, and to ensure that it remains clean. Only gentle movements are allowed for a few days, to give the new cornea time to settle into place. After a few weeks, the patient should usually be able to get back to normal, everyday activities.

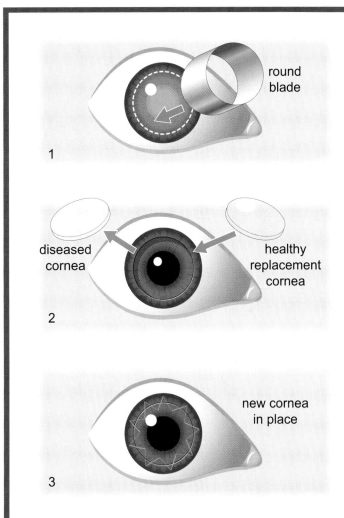

These diagrams show how a corneal transplant is carried out.
1. A disc of the cornea is removed.
2. A disc from the donor cornea is put into the hole.
3. The new cornea is stitched into place.

New corneas

After corneas are removed from a donor, they can be kept in an eye bank for up to a month. They are stored at 2 to 6 degrees Centigrade in a special solution containing chemicals and drugs, which keep the tissue as healthy as possible until the transplant operation. There are not enough corneas available for everybody who needs them, and waiting lists for transplants can be long. Scientists are trying to develop artificial corneas made from plastic to reduce this shortage.

LIGHT AND DARK

Light has to enter the eye in order for us to see anything. Too much light can damage the eye, yet with too little light we cannot see clearly. The eye has its own built-in mechanism for regulating the amount of light that enters it.

The iris

The **iris** is a flattened ring that hangs between the **cornea** and the **lens**. The outer edge of the ring is attached to folds of tissue called ciliary processes, which jut out from the ciliary muscles.

The iris is made up of two sets of muscle fibres:

- radial muscles: these run from the outside edge of the iris towards the centre, like spokes on a bicycle wheel
- circular muscles: these form the inner rim of the iris, and are arranged in a series of rings.

These muscles contract in response to signals from the brain. They are antagonistic muscles, which means that when one contracts, the other relaxes. They are also involuntary muscles – we cannot make them contract by thinking about it. By controlling the size of the iris, they also control the amount of light that enters the eye.

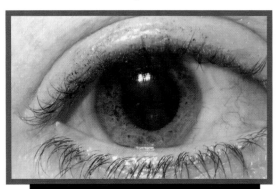

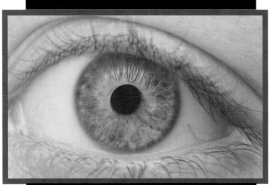

The top photograph is taken in dim light and the bottom in bright light. You can see how the size of the pupil responds to the different light conditions.

Muscle contractions

The radial and circular muscles have opposite effects: when the rings of circular muscles contract, they pull the radial muscles inwards, shrinking the size of the pupil. When the straight radial muscles contract, they pull the circular muscles outwards, enlarging the size of the **pupil**.

In normal light, there is a balance between the two, and the pupil is an in-between size.

In bright light, circular muscles contract to reduce the pupil size and restrict the amount of light entering the eye.

In dim light, radial muscles contract, enlarging the pupil size to allow as much light as possible to enter the eye.

Check it out!

You can see these effects for yourself if you stand in front of a mirror in a bright room. Look carefully at your pupils, then shut your eyes and cover them (without pressing on them.) Open your eyes after a few minutes and stare into the mirror – you should be able to watch your large, dilated pupils shrink rapidly.

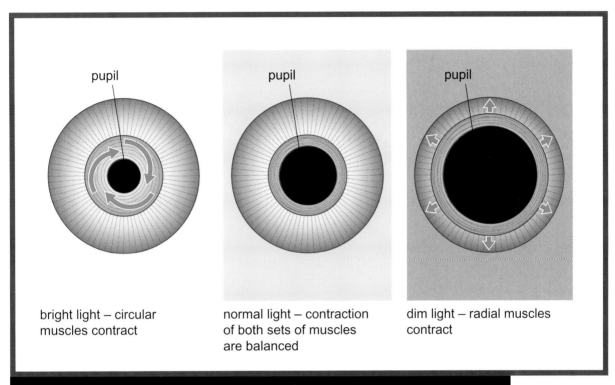

bright light – circular muscles contract

normal light – contraction of both sets of muscles are balanced

dim light – radial muscles contract

These diagrams show how the iris muscles control the size of the pupil.

Drug effects

If an **optician** needs to see clearly into the eye, the normal opening of the pupil may not be enough. They may put a few drops of a drug, called atropine, onto the lower eyelid. As you blink, the atropine is spread across the eyeball, and acts on the muscles of the iris to make them enlarge the pupil completely. The effects of atropine wear off after a few hours and the pupil size goes back to normal.

Some recreational drugs that people take for non-medical reasons may also affect the size of the pupil.

Tears are produced all the time, not just when we cry. They help to keep our eyes moist and clean. Special glands under the eyelids produce the tears. They drain away via the nasal cavity.

This diagram shows the structures that are involved in the production and drainage of tears.

Tear production

Under each upper eyelid is a **lacrimal gland**, which is about the same size and shape as an almond. Each gland produces about 1 millilitre of lacrimal fluid (tears) every day. There are between three and twelve lacrimal ducts, which carry the fluid away from the glands and empty it onto the inside surface of the upper eyelid.

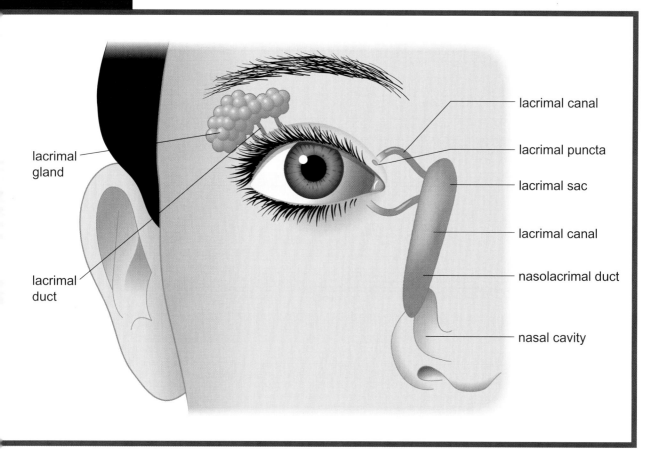

lacrimal gland

lacrimal duct

lacrimal canal

lacrimal puncta

lacrimal sac

lacrimal canal

nasolacrimal duct

nasal cavity

What do tears do?

Tears are a sterile, watery solution that contains salts, mucus and an **enzyme**, called lysozyme. They have four main functions:
- to wash dirt off the surface of the eyeball
- to keep the surface of the eyeball clear and moist
- to carry water and nutrients to the **cornea** and **lens**
- to prevent infection – lysozyme kills bacteria, preventing infection.

Blinking

We blink regularly, usually about once every 4 or 5 seconds, and each blink lasts less than 0.5 seconds. Blinking spreads lacrimal fluid across the surface of the eyeball, and also stimulates the lacrimal glands to produce more lacrimal fluid.

Where do tears go?

Once they have been spread over the eyeball, tears drain away into small openings called lacrimal puncta, at the inner edge of the eye. These drain into the lacrimal canals, and from there the tears flow through the lacrimal sac and nasolacrimal duct into the nasal cavity. They leave the nasal cavity either by draining away down the throat or into a handkerchief when we blow our nose.

The fumes from the cut onion have irritated this person's eyes, stimulating the production of excess tears.

Sometimes, we produce more tears than the drainage system can cope with. If we cry, or if our eyes are producing a lot of tears because of an irritation or allergy, the tears accumulate in our eyes and spill over. Tears also build up if the nose and nasal cavity are blocked, for example, if we have a bad cold, our eyes then tend to be watery because the tears cannot drain away properly.

Crying

The ability to express emotions – such as extreme happiness, extreme sadness and pain or shock – by crying is thought to be unique to humans. No other animals are known to be able to do this.

Reflex tears

Our eyes produce extra tears in response to emergencies. For example, tears are produced in response to fumes from an onion irritating the eye, or the presence of a foreign object in the eye.

Why do your eyes sting at the swimming pool?

Many people find that when they go to an indoor swimming pool, their eyes sting and start to stream. This is because the disinfectants used to keep the water clean contain a chemical called chlorine. It irritates the eyes, making them sting, and extra tears are produced to wash the chlorine away. You do not need to be actually in the water to be affected – some people's eyes produce extra tears in response to chlorine that has evaporated into the warm atmosphere.

INSIDE AN EYE

An adult eyeball is about 2.5 centimetres in diameter, with a complex internal structure. The outside layers enclose hollow spaces filled with liquid and gel. A system of muscles controls the shape of the clear **lens** to focus light rays onto the light-sensitive layer at the back of the eye.

This diagram shows the structures inside an eyeball.

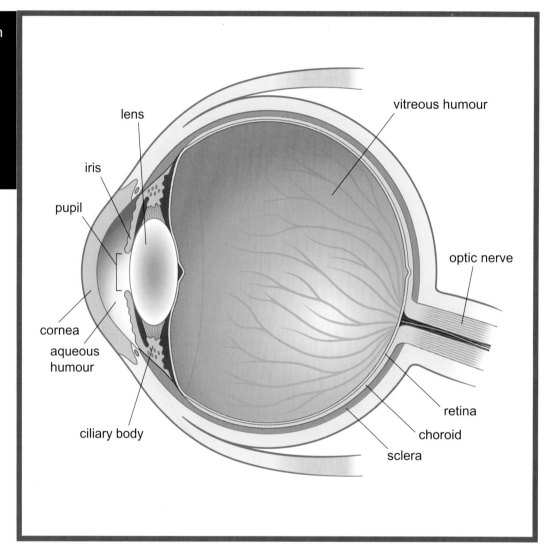

lens

iris

pupil

cornea

aqueous humour

ciliary body

vitreous humour

optic nerve

retina

choroid

sclera

Basic structure

The eyeball has three main layers:

- The **sclera** and **cornea** form the outer, protective layer.
- The middle layer is the choroid, which contains black pigment to prevent light reflecting inside the eye. The choroid has a good blood supply, bringing nutrients to the internal structures of the eye. At the front of the eye, the choroid forms the ciliary body and the **iris**.
- The inner layer is the **retina**, containing light-sensitive cells and nerve cells.

There are two chambers inside the eyeball, one in front of the lens and one behind it. The chamber in front of the lens is filled with a watery liquid, called aqueous humour. This provides nutrients for the cornea and lens, which do not have their own blood supply. The chamber behind the lens is filled with a soft jelly, called vitreous humour. The aqueous and vitreous humours press outwards, helping to maintain the round shape of the eyeball and to prevent it collapsing inwards.

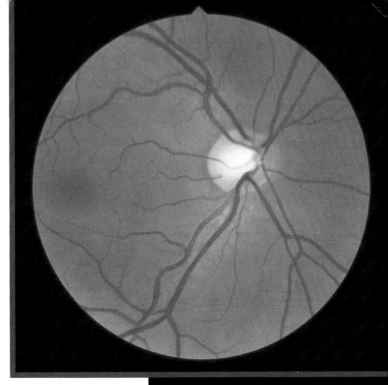

This photograph shows the retina, as an optician would see it using an ophthalmoscope. The fine red lines are blood capillaries.

Ciliary body

The ciliary body lies between the two chambers of the eyeball. It contains a ring of circular muscle, the **ligaments** of which hold the lens in place. By contracting and relaxing, the circular muscle controls the shape of the lens. The ciliary body produces aqueous humour and vitreous humour.

Lens

The lens is a transparent disc made of elastic gel. It bends light rays as they pass through it.

Retina

The retina is the light-sensitive inner layer that covers the back three-quarters of the eyeball. It sends electrical signals to nerves when stimulated by light rays. The retina contains a network of blood **capillaries**, which an **optician** can see when examining the eye. The 'red eye' effect that appears on some flash photographs is caused by reflection of light by these blood capillaries.

Optic nerve

The electrical signals generated by light-sensitive cells in the retina pass to nerve cells and then to the optic nerve. The **optic nerve** carries the signals to the brain.

Moving the eyeball

The eyeball is held in place by six muscles, each attached to the outside of the eyeball and the bones of the skull. They are some of the fastest and most precise muscles in the body, allowing us to move our eyes up and down, and from side to side. A 'squint' or 'lazy eye' may develop if the muscles of the two eyes are unbalanced, or do not work together properly. This is usually noticed when a child is young, and can often be corrected by wearing spectacles.

HOW DO WE SEE?

We see an object when light bounces off it into our eyes. Electrical signals are sent from our eyes to our brain, which interprets the signals so that we 'see' the object. The process is rather like taking a photograph with a camera.

Light rays travel from an object and enter the eye, to form an image on the retina.

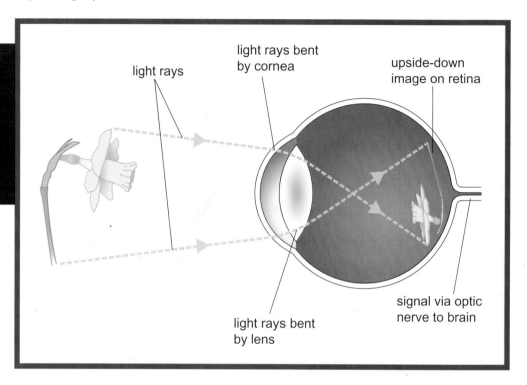

light rays

light rays bent by cornea

upside-down image on retina

light rays bent by lens

signal via optic nerve to brain

There are several stages in the process, as light passes through different structures within the eye.

1 **Cornea:** light rays travel in straight lines from the object to the eye. As they pass through the cornea, the light rays are bent (refracted).

2 **Lens:** the light rays travel through the watery aqueous humour, and through the **pupil** to the lens. The lens bends the light rays even more as they pass through it.

3 **Retina:** the light rays travel through the gel-like vitreous humour, to form an image on the retina. Light-sensitive cells, called photoreceptors, respond when light hits them, and send electrical signals to nerve cells.

4 **Optic nerve:** electrical signals travel from the separate nerve cells to the brain via the optic nerve.

5 **Brain:** the signals from the optic nerve reach the vision centre, a small area at the back of the brain. Information is passed from here to other areas, allowing us to associate what we see with what we already know. An example of this is the primary visual cortex, which may receive signals about a white triangle on a blue background, but our previous experience allows the brain to interpret this as a yacht sail on the sea.

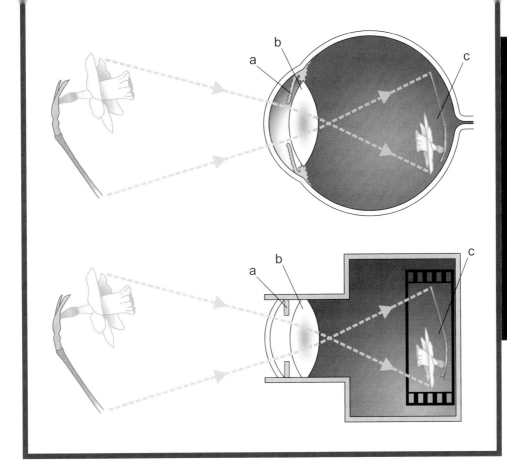

This diagram shows how the eye works in a similar way to a camera:

a) aperture and iris control the amount of light entering
b) lenses bend light rays
c) images focused on film and retina.

Like a camera

You can think of the eye as a sort of biological camera:

	camera	eye
amount of light entering controlled by	aperture	iris
light rays bent by	lens	lens
image focused on	film	retina

Bending light

Light rays travel in straight lines, and can travel more quickly through some materials than others. As light rays pass from air through the more dense cornea, they slow down and are bent. They are bent even more as they pass through the lens. This bending is called **refraction**. Both the cornea and lens make the light rays converge – bend inwards. They continue in straight lines through the vitreous humour, but cross over so that the image that forms on the retina is upside down.

Looking at refraction

If you put a straw in a glass of water and look at it carefully, you will see that the straw seems to bend where it enters the water. Look at it from the other side and it will seem to bend in the opposite direction. This is due to refraction – the light rays travel more quickly through air than through water, so the end of the straw seems to be in the wrong place.

SHORT SIGHT

The medical name for **short sight** is 'myopia', and people who are short-sighted are called 'myopic'. Although they may see things close to them very clearly, they have only a blurred view of things in the distance.

These diagrams show:
a) normal sight
b) light rays in a myopic eye
c) a spectacle lens correcting short sight.

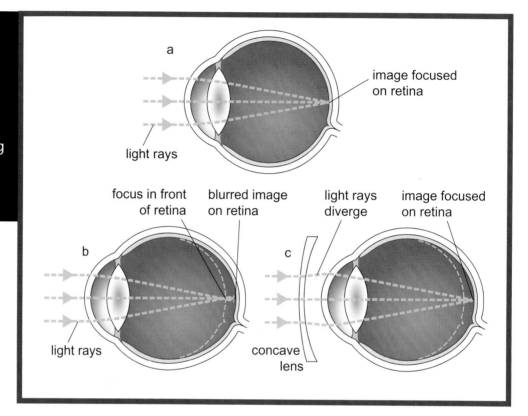

What causes short sight?

There are two main reasons for short sight:

- an eyeball that is too long
- a **lens** that is too thick.

The longer the eyeball, or the thicker the lens, the more short-sighted the person will be.

Inside the eye

Light rays are bent by the **cornea** and the lens. These should focus them so that an image forms on the **retina**. In a short-sighted person, the light rays are focused in front of the retina. An out-of-focus image on the retina means that the person can only see a blurred view.

The problem is worse with objects in the distance, because the light rays are more nearly parallel when they reach the eye; with closer objects, the light rays still diverge.

People who are short-sighted may be able to see things close to them very clearly, but have a blurred view of things in the distance. They normally need to wear glasses or contact lenses for activities such as watching television, looking at a classroom board and driving.

Correcting short sight

Short sight can be corrected with glasses or contact lenses. The light rays are bent outwards by a concave lens before they reach the eye, so that the image is focused perfectly onto the retina by the eye itself. In physics, you may have discovered that a lens of this shape ((will make light rays diverge, but this type of lens is not used to make glasses. Instead, a ((shape lens is used. The lens is thinnest at the centre, and becomes thicker towards the edges.

Treating short sight

Laser treatment may be available for some short-sighted people. This involves using a laser beam to alter the curve of the front of the cornea to make the image focus on the retina. Although this treatment has had some success, the changes are not reversible, and some people are concerned about taking any risk with the eye.

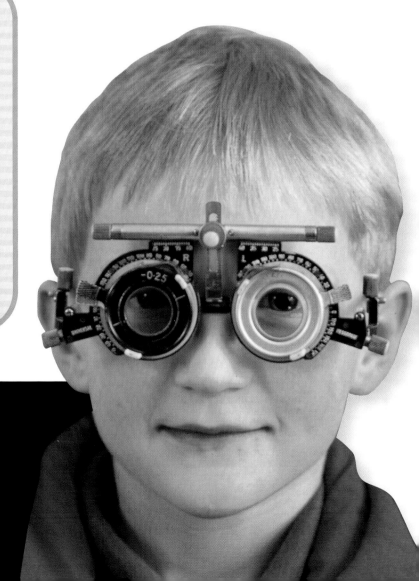

In an eye test, these special glasses are to test how well a person can see the letters on an eye chart. A person with normal sight would see the letters clearly. To a short-sighted person, they would appear blurred.

LONG SIGHT

The medical name for **long sight** is 'hypermetropia', and people who are long-sighted are called 'hypermetropic'. This means that although they may see things very clearly in the distance, they have a blurred view of things close to them.

What causes long sight?

Long sight is the opposite of short sight. The causes are the opposite, too:

- an eyeball that is too short
- a **lens** that is too thin.

The shorter the eyeball, or the thinner the lens, the more long-sighted the person will be.

Inside the eye

In a long-sighted person, the light rays are not focused on the **retina**. The actual point of focus is further away than the retina, so a blurred image forms on the retina.

The problem is worse with close objects because the light rays are still diverging when they reach the eye; with more distant objects, the light rays are more nearly parallel.

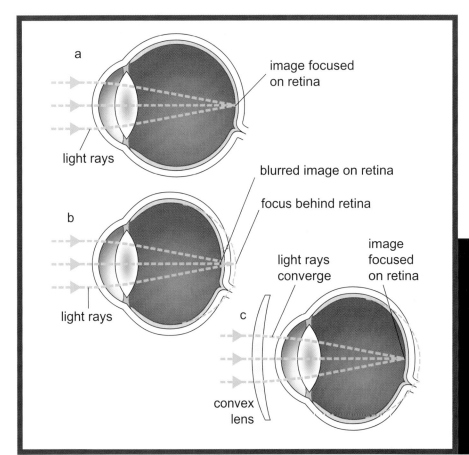

a
image focused on retina
light rays

blurred image on retina
focus behind retina
b
light rays

light rays converge
image focused on retina
c
convex lens

These diagrams show:
a) normal sight
b) light rays in a long-sighted eye
c) a spectacle lens correcting the long sight.

People who are long-sighted may be able to see things in the distance very clearly, but have a blurred view of things closer to them. They normally need to wear glasses or contact lenses for activities such as reading and writing.

Correcting long sight

Convex lenses are used to correct long sight. The lens is thickest at the centre and becomes thinner towards the edges. The lens makes the light rays converge, so that the image is focused onto the retina.

Astigmatism

Many people's eyes have an **astigmatism**. This means that the curve of the **cornea** or lens is uneven. Some parts of the image will be focused perfectly on the retina, but other parts of the image will not. This gives a rather blurred and distorted view of everything.

Astigmatism can usually be corrected by lenses that bend light more in one direction than in another. However, some astigmatisms are so severe that they cannot be fully corrected.

A person with normal sight would see their writing clearly.

NEAR AND FAR

You can see things that are close to you – like this book. You can also look out of a window and see things that are in the distance. The adjustment that our eyes make to allow us to see things both near and far is called 'accommodation'.

Focusing light rays

For a clear image, light rays must be focused.

In a camera, light rays are focused by lenses to make an image on the film. The distance between the **lens** and the image is called the **focal length**. An ordinary camera has just one, unchangeable lens. It will always focus light rays in the same way, and so will always take the same kind of picture. Lenses are usually set to take clear pictures several metres away from the camera, and so objects much closer than that tend to be fuzzy and blurred. This is because light rays from distant objects travel almost parallel to each other and only need to be bent a little to focus them. Light rays from closer objects diverge (move away from each other). To be focused, they either need to be bent more, or they need a greater focal length.

Professional photographers can change the lenses on their cameras to focus the light in different ways. This helps them to take pictures of both very close and very distant objects. To focus closer objects, they use a fatter lens that will bend light rays more, or a lens with a longer focal length.

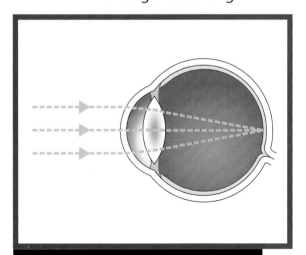

When we look at something in the distance, the light rays are nearly parallel. The lens is thin and flat because it does not need to bend the light rays much to focus them onto the retina.

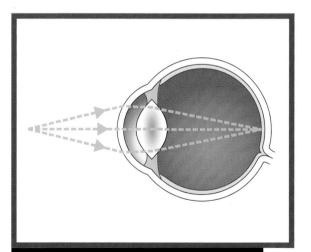

When we look at something close to our eyes, the light rays are diverging. The lens needs to be thicker and fatter to focus the light rays onto the retina.

In our eyes

We cannot alter the focal length inside our eyes, nor can we swap a lens for a different one. Instead, some very precise adjustments take place inside our eyes.

The lens is held in place inside the eye by **ligaments** attached to ciliary muscles. When we look at things in the distance, the ciliary muscle relaxes and the suspensory ligaments pull on the lens, making it thin and flat. This reduces its bending power, so that it brings the parallel light rays to a perfect focus on the **retina**.

An ordinary camera has a fixed lens. It can focus things in the distance, as the light rays are nearly parallel. Objects closer to it will be fuzzy and blurred, because it cannot focus the diverging light rays onto the film.

When we look at things closer to us, the ciliary muscle contracts, which makes the suspensory ligaments relax. As the lens becomes fatter and more convex, its bending power increases, and it is able to focus the diverging light rays perfectly on the retina.

If we look at objects at an in-between distance, the muscles and ligaments will pull the lens to an in-between thickness, again focusing the light rays onto the retina.

How close can we see things?

The smallest distance from the eye at which an object can be seen clearly is called the 'near point'. In healthy young adults, this distance is usually about 10 centimetres.

As we age

As people get older, their lens becomes less elastic and the range of vision that it can accommodate decreases. This is called 'presbyopia'. Older people find it harder and harder to read print at the same distance as they could when they were younger. By the age of 40, the near point may be 20 centimetres, increasing to 80 centimetres by the age of 60. Many people overcome this problem by wearing reading glasses. Others choose to wear bifocals – spectacles that have lenses with separate areas for distance vision and reading.

RETINA

The **retina** is the light-sensitive layer that lines the inside of the eyeball. When light falls on the cells of the retina, they respond by sending electrical signals to **optic nerve** cells within the retina. These pass the signals on to the brain.

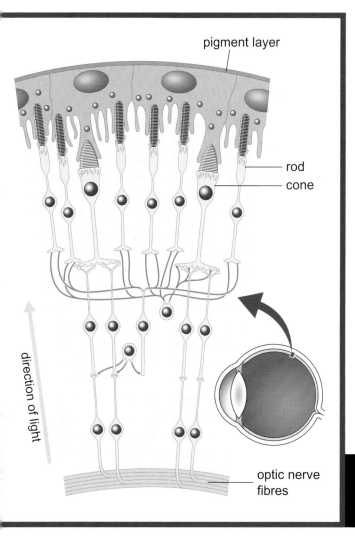

pigment layer

rod

cone

direction of light

optic nerve fibres

Cells of the retina

The retina is mainly made up of neurons (nerve cells) and photoreceptors (light-sensitive cells). At the back of the retina is a layer of cells that contain a black pigment; this absorbs light to stop reflections bouncing around inside the eyeball. There are two types of photoreceptor:

• **rods** allow us to see in dim light; they do not distinguish between different wavelengths of light, so when the light is dim, we can only see shades of grey. They get their name from their long, thin shape. At the tip of each rod is a stack of about 2000 disks containing rhodopsin, the chemical that absorbs light. Each retina contains about 120 million rods.

This diagram shows the arrangement of the cells of the retina.

Colour vision

There are three different types of cone, each containing a different light-absorbing chemical (photopigment). One is sensitive to red light, one to green light and the other to blue light. Our brains distinguish different colours by processing information about the relative numbers of each type of cone that have been stimulated. Looking at a red tomato will stimulate mainly red cones, looking at green grass will stimulate mainly green cones and looking at blue sky will stimulate mainly blue cones. Light that contains a mixture of colours will stimulate some of each type of cone. White light stimulates all three types equally.

- **Cones** can only work in brighter light; they distinguish between different wavelengths of light to allow us to see in colour. They get their name because they are shorter and fatter than rods and the tips are a cone-shape. At the tip of each cone is a folded coil that contains light-absorbing chemicals. Each retina contains about 6.5 million cones.

Parts of the retina

The exact centre of the retina is called the **macula lutea**. This has a small dip in the centre called the fovea, where only cones appear. It is the part of the retina where images are sharpest – when you move your eyes and head to see something clearly, you are trying to centre the image on the fovea.

The point where the optic nerve leaves the retina is called the **blind spot**. There are no rods or cones there, so we cannot see an image that is focused onto it. We are not normally aware it is there, but you can prove it exists. Try this experiment to do so. With your right eye closed, look at the web below. If you change the distance between the book and your eye, you will find a point at which the spider disappears: at that point, the image of the spider falls on the blind spot.

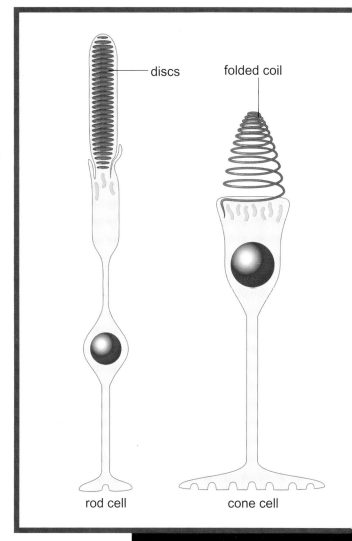

These diagrams show a rod cell and a cone cell. You can see the pile of discs at the tip of the rod and the folded coil at the tip of the cone.

Detached retina
Normally, there is no space between the retina and the other layers of the eyeball. However, sometimes these may become separated, causing a detached retina. This is most common after a head injury or severe jolt, usually caused by sporting activities. The damage can often be successfully repaired by laser treatment or surgery. People who have had a detached retina are often advised to avoid impact sports, such as jogging on hard surfaces and rugby, to prevent any further damage.

COLOUR BLINDNESS

Most people are able to detect differences between a whole range of colours. People who can detect no colour, or a limited range of colours, are said to be colour-blind.

Why are some people colour-blind?

Colour blindness usually occurs because one of the three cone photopigments of the eye is absent. The most common form of colour blindness is 'red-green' – the inability to distinguish between red and green. This is caused by a deficiency in the red or the green cones; as a result, red and green are seen as the same colour. If there are no red cones, red and green will both be seen as green. If there are no green cones, red and green will both be seen as red. Some people suffer from other forms of colour blindness, such as blue-yellow, but this is much rarer.

An inherited condition

Red-green colour blindness is an inherited condition, passed on from one generation to the next. Humans have 23 pairs of chromosomes, containing all the genetic information. Males and females have 22 pairs of chromosomes that are the same, but the last pair are different: females have two X chromosomes, and males have one X and one Y chromosome. The **gene** controlling red-green colour blindness is **only** on the X chromosome. A gene for normal colour vision will always dominate the gene for colour blindness.

These diagrams show how red-green colour blindness is inherited.

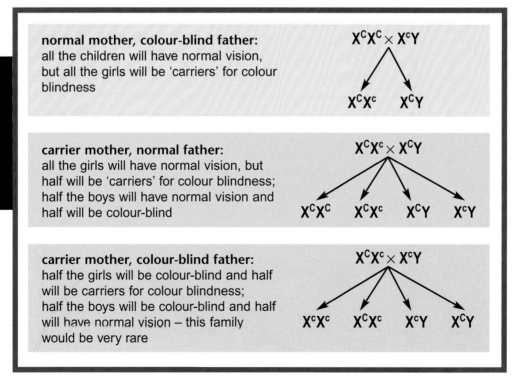

normal mother, colour-blind father: all the children will have normal vision, but all the girls will be 'carriers' for colour blindness

$$X^C X^C \times X^c Y$$
$$X^C X^c \qquad X^C Y$$

carrier mother, normal father: all the girls will have normal vision, but half will be 'carriers' for colour blindness; half the boys will have normal vision and half will be colour-blind

$$X^C X^c \times X^C Y$$
$$X^C X^C \qquad X^C X^c \qquad X^C Y \qquad X^c Y$$

carrier mother, colour-blind father: half the girls will be colour-blind and half will be carriers for colour blindness; half the boys will be colour-blind and half will have normal vision – this family would be very rare

$$X^C X^c \times X^c Y$$
$$X^c X^c \qquad X^C X^c \qquad X^C Y \qquad X^c Y$$

male		female	
X^CY	normal vision	X^CX^C	normal vision
X^cY	colour-blind	X^CX^c	normal vision, but Xc carrier
		X^cX^c	colour-blind

Red-green colour blindness affects 8 per cent of men, but only 0.4 per cent of women. This is because we only inherit one chromosome from each parent. A girl has two X chromosomes, so to be colour-blind she must inherit X^c from both her father and her mother; a boy has only one X chromosome, so to be colour-blind he only needs to inherit X^c from his mother. The table above shows the different possibilities.

Testing for colour blindness

People are usually tested for colour blindness by using Ishihara test cards. These are covered in patterns of dots of various shades. People with normal vision will see numbers in the patterns of dots. Colour-blind people see only a random pattern of dots, because they cannot distinguish between the colours.

Cards like these may be used to test for colour blindness. People with normal vision will see the number or pattern, but colour-blind people will just see random dots.

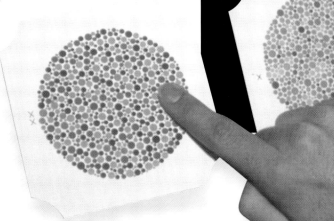

Living with colour blindness

Being colour-blind may give a slightly strange view of the world but, because a colour-blind person has never known anything else, they have nothing with which to compare it. There can be difficulties in everyday situations – for example, someone who is red-green colour-blind cannot tell the difference between red and green traffic lights. Instead, they have to rely on the position of the lights on the pole. They may also be unable to do some jobs where these colours need to be distinguished, for example, a train driver, a pilot or snooker player.

EYE EXAMINATIONS

Even if you are not experiencing any difficulties or problems with your eyes, it is important to have them examined regularly. Any problems that may be developing can be detected very early – and the sooner they are, the sooner they can be put right! Eye examinations can sometimes detect signs of disease elsewhere in the body, and your **optician** can refer you to a doctor, if necessary.

How often do you need an eye test?

Some people need to visit an optician more frequently than others. As soon as you were born, your eyes were probably examined by a doctor, followed by another check at about six months. Most pre-school children have an eye check, and regular checks follow every few years throughout your school life.

If you are having any problems – headaches, difficulty reading, seeing in the distance or blurred vision, you should arrange to see an optician.

If you already wear glasses or contact lenses, your optician will tell you how often you need to have your prescription checked. Some people's sight stays stable for a long time, while other people experience periods during which their vision changes rapidly.

What does an optician do?

The optician will carry out several different tests; the exact tests may depend on any problems you are having. Some of the equipment may look rather complicated, but there is nothing to worry about – the tests do not hurt at all.

Distance vision can be checked by asking you to read a series of letters from a chart at some distance from you. Near vision can be checked by asking you to read different sizes of print held at arm's length.

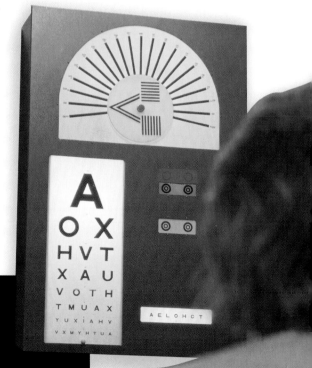

A chart similar to this may be used to test how good your distance vision is.

Looking at patterns on different backgrounds can help the optician find out whether you have an **astigmatism**.

The pressure inside each eyeball may be tested by directing a puff of air at the front of each eye – this may make you blink, but it does not hurt. High pressure in the eye may indicate glaucoma; this is a major cause of blindness, and its early detection is very important.

The optician may want to see inside your eye, using a torch to shine a tiny beam of bright light into your eye; a larger piece of equipment may also be used, with a chin rest and a frame to help you to keep your head still. For a more detailed examination, the optician may want to put some drops into your eye. This makes the **pupil** dilate, which gives a clear view inside. Your vision may be blurry for a while afterwards, but it will soon return to normal.

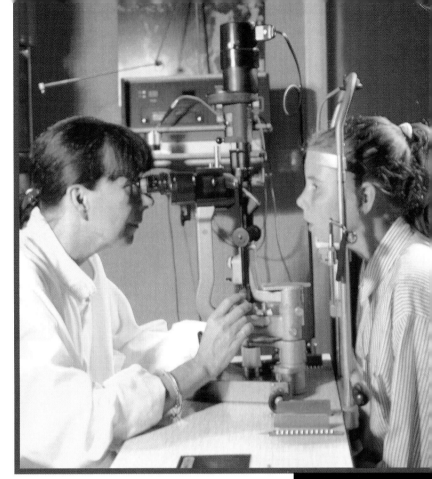

This optician is examining the inside of the patient's eye, to make sure everything is healthy.

Prescribing spectacles

Once the optician has done all the tests, it may be decided that your vision would be improved by wearing spectacles. Using an adjustable frame, the optician can try out different lenses, in slightly different positions, until exactly the right prescription is found for you.

Choosing and fitting spectacles

It is important that your spectacles fit you properly and that the lenses are correctly lined up with your eyes. Today, there are many different styles and types to choose from, and many different types of lenses, too. You might prefer contact lenses instead and, again, there is a lot of choice, so listen to any advice your optician offers you.

Spectacles and sport

If you play sport, there are many special types of safety spectacles and protective goggles that you can wear. Find out what is suitable for your sport, and make sure you wear them whenever you play.

USING BOTH EYES

We see the world around us in three dimensions – things have height, width and depth. We can also judge the distances between objects. This is only possible because each of our eyes has a slightly different view of things.

When you look at an object, you see the same object with both eyes. However, the left eye will see a view a little to the left of the view the right eye sees. Each eye sends a slightly different signal to the brain. When it puts the two sets of signals together, the brain is able to interpret the information, and we see a three-dimensional view of the object.

When you look at an object close to you, each eye has to turn inwards towards your nose. The brain receives signals from stretch-receptors in the eye muscles, giving it information about how much each eye has turned inwards. The brain uses this information to work out how far away the object is. The more the muscles are stretched, the more the eyes are turned inwards, and so the nearer the object must be.

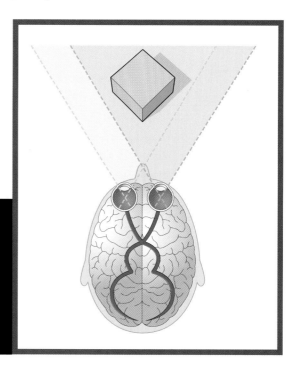

In this diagram, the blue triangle shows the area seen by the left eye, and the pink triangle shows the area seen by the right eye. When the brain receives this information, it interprets it and you see the balanced, three-dimensional view of the cube.

Different views

As the diagram shows, each eye sees a different area. The position of the eyes in the head affects how much these areas overlap, and therefore affects the overall view that is seen. Animals, such as rabbits, which are likely to be the prey of other animals, have their eyes at the sides of their heads, giving them the widest possible view. Animals that are predators have eyes at the front of their heads, limiting their sideways vision but increasing the accuracy of their forward vision.

Judging distance

Judging shape and distance is important in many aspects of our everyday lives. We need to be able to judge how far away from our feet a step is, and when we put out our hand, we expect to be able to pick up a drink without thinking about how far away the mug is.

Judging shape, space and distance is vital for drivers and for sports players, too. A tennis player, for example, needs to be able to pinpoint accurately the position of the ball, the racquet and the lines on the court.

Peripheral vision

Usually, we look straight ahead and have a view of what is in front of us. Our eyes also collect information from each side. This is called 'peripheral vision'. Good forward vision is essential in animals that hunt, enabling them to see their prey very clearly. Animals that are hunted usually have eyes at the side of their heads, giving them good all round vision for spotting predators. Humans have a field of vision of about 200 degrees – about 100 degrees on each side of the nose. You can test this by looking straight ahead, holding up one hand and moving it slowly backwards – it will probably disappear from sight just before it is level with your ears. Detecting movement to each side helps us to keep safe, especially when driving or crossing a busy road. It is also important in some sports, alerting the player so that he can react rapidly. Some people suffer from a condition called 'tunnel vision'. This is a condition in which their peripheral vision is extremely restricted – their view of the world is simply like looking through a narrow tunnel. This can make some activities very difficult for them.

The brain uses the information from both eyes to enable this tennis player to judge distances accurately.

One eye

Some people can cope extremely well with only one eye. They may have perfect colour vision, and be able to see outlines and details very clearly. However, they find it very difficult to judge three-dimensional shapes and distances, because their brain receives only one image and has nothing with which to compare it.

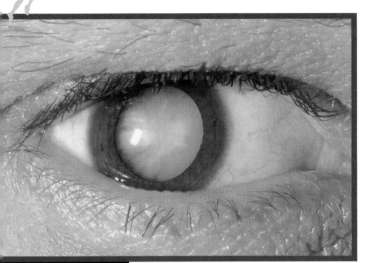

Cataracts make this person's eyes look cloudy and white.

Cataracts

The formation of cataracts is one of the most common causes of blindness. The **lens** gradually changes from being clear and transparent to being cloudy and opaque. The quality of the person's vision slowly deteriorates until, eventually, they become completely blind.

Cataracts are usually thought to occur in elderly people, but they can also develop in people with diabetes and other illnesses. Exposure to ultra-violet light, long-term use of some drugs and smoking are also thought to be involved in cataract formation.

Changing spectacle prescriptions can help in the early stages but, as the lens becomes increasingly opaque, there will come a point where no further improvement can be made.

Glaucoma

This condition mainly affects people over the age of 40, and is more common in women than in men. It tends to run in families, and scientists think that there is a genetic link. Glaucoma occurs when the fluid inside the eye does not drain away properly. As more fluid is made, the pressure inside the eye increases. At high pressure, the nerve cells of the retina may become damaged, and the person's vision deteriorates. In most people, the process is slow and painless.

Cataract surgery

Cataract surgery is routinely carried out, often under local anaesthetic, with the patient in hospital as a day patient or overnight. The damaged lens is removed, and a new, plastic lens inserted in its place. The patient's sight is fully restored within a few days; spectacles may be needed to make minor adjustments, but the person's sight is often much better than it ever was.

Trachoma

This is the greatest single cause of blindness in the world, and affects more than 150 million people. A micro-organism, *Chlamydia trachomatis,* infects the eye. It causes conjunctivitis, and leads to the growth of extra tissue and blood vessels in the **cornea**. Slowly, the cornea becomes opaque and the patient loses their sight. It is easily passed from one person to another, and is also spread by flies. Trachoma is most common in countries without reliable sanitation.

Although the **antibiotics** needed to treat trachoma are relatively cheap and available in much of the world, they are often prohibitively expensive and scarce amongst those people who are most at risk. By improving sanitation and water supplies, and by introducing drug distribution programmes, the World Health Organization is attempting to eradicate the disease completely by 2020.

Macular degeneration

The central area of the retina is called the **macula lutea**. As people age, this can slowly break down. This causes blurred and distorted vision, and can eventually lead to complete blindness. The breakdown of the macula may be caused by blood leaking from **capillaries**, and laser treatment can often prevent further leakage, halting any further loss of vision. However, in some cases, the lining of the retina starts to break down. Until recently, this has been untreatable, but current research indicates that some drugs may help. Tiny computer implants are also being developed to restore some vision.

Diabetic retinopathy

Some people who have had diabetes for many years may develop this condition, in which high blood sugar levels make blood vessels in the retina swell and leak blood. This can lead to blurred vision, blind spots and 'floaters'. As the disease advances, the retina becomes scarred, and vision deteriorates further. Regulating the blood sugar level and controlling blood pressure can both help to reduce the risk of developing diabetic retinopathy. Laser treatment may be used to seal blood vessels, and scientists are developing new drugs to help with blood vessel growth and repair.

This photomicrograph shows the retina of an eye in which macular degeneration is advanced. The second picture shows how vision is affected.

People may be blind for different reasons, but they all have the same problem – how to cope with everyday life and living. Many things are available to help blind people, and modern technology is providing more all the time.

Why are people blind?

There are many different causes of blindness. Some people are blind at birth, perhaps because of a genetic defect or an infection during the mother's pregnancy. Some may have an illness or disease that slowly destroys their sight; others may lose their sight suddenly due to an accident. Some drugs and chemicals can also lead to blindness.

Blindness may be due to damage to the eye itself, to the **optic nerves** that link the eyes and brain or to the areas of the brain that are involved in receiving and interpreting the signals from the eyes.

The Braille alphabet allows blind people to read and write.

Braille

In the early nineteenth century, a blind Frenchman named Louis **Braille** developed an alphabet of raised dots. For the first time, blind people could 'read' by feeling the patterns of dots. They could also 'write' by using a pointed tool to prick out their own patterns of dots on paper.

This system was called 'Braille', after its inventor. The first Braille book was published in 1827; now, the system has spread almost worldwide, and has been adapted to virtually every language. Braille machines can be used to type Braille messages.

What can blind people see?

For some blind people, the world is completely black and dark; they cannot see any shape, movement or light. Other blind people do have a small amount of vision – perhaps just a shadowy awareness of light and dark, or the ability to detect some movements around them.

Blind or partially sighted?

A person with normal, healthy eyes is said to have '20/20 vision'. This means that, at a distance of 20 feet, they can read clearly what should normally be seen at that distance. If, for example, a **short-sighted** person had 20/40 vision, they would see at 20 feet what a person with normal vision would see at 40 feet. To be classified as legally blind in the United Kingdom, a person's vision has to be 3/60 or worse – in other words, at 3 feet or less they see what a person with normal vision would see at 60 feet. Between 3/60 and 6/60, a person is classed as partially sighted. The exact level of vision for a person to be classed as blind differs slightly from one country to another.

Communication

Most people read regularly, for pleasure, for work and for finding information and news. We read books, newspapers, magazines, computer screens, signs and maps. We also write notes, cheques, essays, letters and e-mails. If you are blind, it is difficult to receive and send information in any of these ways.

Louis Braille was born in 1809 and died in 1852.

LIVING WITH BLINDNESS

Reading and writing are not the only problems that blind people face. They need to be able to live satisfying and independent lives, and to be safe at home and outside. Many things are available to help blind people to achieve this – and many blind people are extremely successful in what they do.

Getting around

For many years, blind people relied upon tapping a cane in front and to each side to help them to find their way along pavements. In the early twentieth century, the first guide dogs were trained to help blind people to find their way around more easily and safely. Today, guide dogs provide invaluable help and support for many blind people. **Braille** and talking compasses can help with navigation; another type of device can be worn around the neck, giving a bleep or vibration when there is an obstruction ahead.

This blind lady relies on her guide dog to navigate her safely wherever she goes.

Helpful gadgets

Gadgets around the home make many tasks easier for blind people. Liquid level indicators fit over the edge of a cup and bleep when liquid touches them. This helps the person to tell when the cup is full. Larger versions fit over a bathtub so that the person knows when to turn off the taps. Talking watches and clocks tell the time; vibrating alarm watches provide a silent way of keeping track of the time. Other talking devices, such as scales for food measurement and thermometers for temperature control, help with tasks we all do without thinking. Plastic covers for the ends of keys can have raised dots, like Braille, making it simple to find the right key.

Being blind should not mean that you cannot go out and enjoy yourself. Places like concert halls often now have seat numbers in Braille, to help blind people find the right seat. Theatres usually have audio facilities, so that the person can hear a description of what is happening on stage while they listen to the actors' voices.

Blind children

At one time, blind children were trained to do only boring jobs – things that they could do without needing to see. Their education was often limited, and they were not expected to achieve much, if any, personal success. However, blind children have ambitions just like everybody else in our society and, with the right help and support, they can achieve them. Perhaps the biggest handicap for blind people is not the blindness itself, but the negative attitudes of other people around them.

Modern technology

Modern technology has provided some sophisticated equipment to help blind people. Closed circuit televisions (CCTV) make it possible for many partially sighted people to read. Simply put the book, birthday card, picture, medicine label or whatever you want to read under a camera. An image is then sent to a television monitor and magnified many times. Some people link this system to a computer, which allows them to access the Internet.

David Blunkett is a British politician. When he was just four years old, he was sent to a special boarding school for blind children. He was elected to Parliament in 1987, and has had important roles in the Government. He has a tremendous memory, and listens to debates in Parliament with his guide dog at his feet.

Marla Runyan competed in the Olympic Games in Sydney, despite being blind.

Marla Runyan

Marla Runyan is an athlete who competed in the Olympic Games in Sydney in 2000. Any athlete who reaches Olympic standards must be considered highly successful – but the amazing thing about Marla Runyan is that her eyesight began to deteriorate when she was nine, and she is now blind! She has only a very small amount of vision remaining, and is only able to read things using a CCTV and computer. Instead of giving up and doing nothing, she has worked hard and achieved success in her sport – she even says that she does not consider her blindness to be a handicap when she is running, because she can remember what the running tracks used to look like!

WHAT CAN GO WRONG WITH MY EYES?

This book has explained the different parts of human eyes, why they are important and how they can be damaged by injury and illness. This page summarizes some of the problems that can affect young peoples' eyes. It also gives you information about how each problem is treated.

Many problems can be avoided or prevented by good health behaviour. This is called prevention. Taking regular exercise and getting plenty of rest are important, as is eating a balanced diet. The table tells you some of the ways you can prevent injury and illness.

Remember, if you think something is wrong with your body, you should always talk to a trained medical professional, like a doctor or a school nurse. Regular medical check-ups are an important part of maintaining a healthy body.

Illness or injury	Cause	Symptoms	Prevention	Treatment
astigmatism	uneven curve of **cornea** or **lens**	blurred and distorted vision	no proven method of prevention	corrective lenses may be used to reduce distortion and improve vision
conjunctivitis	infection or irritation e.g. by cigarette smoke	discomfort, watery eye, sticky fluid around eye	good standard of personal hygiene	depends on cause, but **antibiotics** may be used to clear up infection
detached **retina**	often severe jolt or blow to the head	vision distorted by flashing lights and floaters, sometimes temporary blindness in affected eye	avoidance of situations where head may suffer blows or injury	surgical repair, often using laser
longsightedness	eyeball too long or lens too strong	blurred close-up vision	no proven method of prevention	corrective lenses may be prescribed to improve close-up vision

Illness or injury	Cause	Symptoms	Prevention	Treatment
shortsightedness	eyeball too short or lens too strong	blurred distance vision	no proven method of prevention	corrective lenses may be prescribed to improve distance vision
snowblindness	over-exposure to UV radiation from Sun and reflected by snow	sensitivity to light, pain, headache, redness and swelling of eye and area around eye, dizziness	for skiing or other winter sports, wear goggles or sunglasses that are 100% UVA and UVB protective	cover eyes with cold compress, stay in darkened room, painkillers may be prescribed to reduce pain

 MORE BOOKS TO READ

Five Senses: Open Your Eyes, Discover Your Sense of Sight, Vivki Cobb and Cynthia Copeland Lewis (Millbrook Press, 2002)

Sense and Sensors: Seeing, Alvin Silverstein, Virginia Silverstein and Laura Silverstein Nunn (Twenty First Century Books, 2001)

Explore Your Senses: Sight, Laurence P. Pringle (Marshall Cavendish Corporation, 1999)

The 3-D Library of the Human Body: The Eye, Learning How We See, Jennifer Viegas (Rosen Publishing Group, 2001)

Bodyworks: Eyes, Katherine Goode (Blackbirch Press, 2000)

Human Body: Eyes, Robert James (Rourke Publishing Group, 1995)

# GLOSSARY

accommodation changes that take place inside the eye to allow us to see close and distant objects clearly

antibiotics drugs used to fight infections. They destroy micro-organisms such as bacteria or fungi, but are not effective against viruses

astigmatism uneven curve of the cornea or lens

blind spot point where the optic nerve leaves the retina

Braille alphabet of raised dots that allows blind people to 'read'

capillary very fine blood vessel

colour blindness inability to detect differences between colours

cones cells in the retina that are responsible for colour vision

conjunctiva delicate outer layer of the eye

cornea transparent layer at the front of the eye

embryo unborn child that is still developing and growing inside the mother's body

enzyme protein that acts as a catalyst in chemical reactions

focal length distance between a lens and the image

gene tiny part of a chromosome that controls one particular characteristic

immune system body's defence mechanisms against infection and disease

iris coloured, muscular ring at the centre of the eye

lacrimal gland place where tears are produced

lens jelly-like disc that bends light entering the eye

ligaments strong cords that bind body structures together

local anaesthetic drug given to numb a part of the body

long sight (longsightedness) condition in which a person can see distant things clearly, but close things appear blurred

macula lutea sensitive central area of the retina

melanin pigment that gives the iris its colour

membrane thin covering layer of tissue

optic nerve nerve that carries electrical signals from the retina to the brain

optician person who examines eyes

pupil hole at the front of the eye through which light enters the eye

radiation energy waves that may be harmful

refraction bending of light as it passes through different materials

retina light-sensitive layer at the back of the eye

rods cells in the retina that are responsible for vision in dim light

sclera white surface layer of the eye

short sight (shortsightedness) condition in which a person can see close things clearly, but distant things appear blurred

virus microbe that uses the body's own cells to make copies of itself

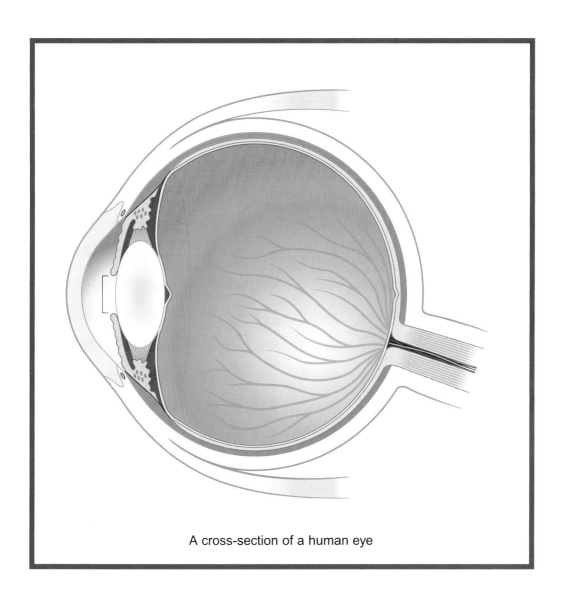

A cross-section of a human eye

INDEX

Books are to be returned on or before
the last date below.

6128